Praise for Ty Garth

For almost 20 years and counting, I've watched TyJuan Garth grow tremendously. His thirst for our people to be successful and prosperous in their own right strikes a match in me personally to want to be an even better member of society! Growing up in some of the worst environments like many of us did, Ty has managed to turn all the personal anguish and heartache into a flower of positivity filled with love and optimism for all. This book is a dose of daily strength and encouragement that Ty feeds to everyone who crosses his path.

— Dred Yehudah
Cofounder of OllieLife Youth Program

Ty Garth has always been a person of faith, a leader, and a being of change and opportunity for his friends, family and for the youth. Ty is a person I've always admired for being a true friend who will give his last for those in need. He has always had an entrepreneurial mindset despite the circumstance being presented to him as a kid and throughout our childhood. Ty has a great passion for our youth and for their development and growth. He desires to show kids there is always another way to think to process information and to rise above your circumstance—a trait that has been instilled in him by his mother who worked hard and sacrificed so much to pour into her kids and to her family so that they could have opportunities. Ty has had tremendous support, and the reason he pours his heart into others is to pay the gift of love forward. His biggest gift is his son, Caleb, that following in his footsteps becomes a great child of faith and service.

—*Derron Ragland*
Vice President of OllieLife Youth Program

OLLIEISM

PART 2

TYJUAN GARTH

WWW.TRUEVINEPUBLISHING.ORG

OLLIEISM
Tyjuan Garth

Published by
True Vine Publishing Co.
810 Dominican Dr.
Nashville, TN 37228
www.TrueVinePublishing.org

Printed in the United States of America—First printing.

Dedication Page

Nipsey Hussle's profound statement that the "highest act of kindness is to inspire" resonates deeply with me. I have dedicated myself to inspiring my family, my son, friends, and the youth I serve. Acknowledging that this endeavor requires support, I have sought mentorship from respected men within the community. We are the foundation upon which our culture's success is built. To effect change, we must be the catalysts, and that transformation begins with self-love. OLLIEISM offers a daily reminder of our inherent excellence, encouraging us to embody our authentic selves, as ordained by God.

This book is dedicated to my Heavenly Father for his undying love for me. Thank you, Lord. My mother, Regina Garth, who has been my inspiration since the day I was born, I love you more than words can express. Thank you. To Lamont, Foni, Floyd, and Leco. Thank you for always pushing me to be great. Caleb TyJuan Garth, my amazingly wonderful son, when God gifted me with you, life changed. You have made me the greatest father ever, and I love you with every ounce of me. Thank you for being such an inspiration. To my Rosa's/924 family - cousins (R.I.P. Asia), aunts, uncles, nephews, nieces, etc. - thank you for always believing in me and supporting me. I love you all to the moon and back. Family over everything is our motto. To my brothers from another mother - Derron, Dred, Nell, Devon, Jeff, Trae, Ahmaad (RIP), Victor (RIP), Fred, Jay, Jermaine, Jeremy, Tyrone, and Deneshia (sister from another mister) - my love and heart are indebted to you all forever. Lastly, to my father, Leroy Bonner, we may not have been in a great space for most of my life, and that's okay because I've had amazing men step in to mentor me, like Dr. Larry Glover and Jesse Calico, but you are my father. I appreciate your absence and your presence because it played a part in me becoming the man I am today. Thank you! "Only Living Life In Excellence"

Introduction

I am Ty Garth, co-founder of Ollie Lifestyle LLC, and I am pleased to present the second installment of OLLIEISM. This time, I would like to share more affirmations that have helped me navigate life's challenges. I also wish to acknowledge my growth as a man by recognizing my father's impact on my life, despite his absence during my formative years. As a man of faith, I believe it is essential to acknowledge his influence. This second installment focuses on forgiving my past self and embracing my true identity. I hope readers of this book will be inspired and blessed. Thank you.

OLLIEISM #1

As you celebrate life's joys, reflect on the pains that made those moments more precious.

———————————————✳———————————————

_____

_____

_____

_____

_____

_____

_____

_____

_____

_____

_____

_____

_____

✦ OLLIEISM #2 ✦

Darkness is merely a preparatory phase, enabling us to cherish the forthcoming light. Thus, we should not underestimate the value of anything.

_____

_____

_____

_____

_____

_____

_____

_____

_____

_____

_____

_____

_____

_____

✦ OLLIEISM #3 ✦

God has thoughtfully designed each of us in our own special way. He skillfully made us through His eyes, crafting perfectly imperfect children. So appreciate the skin you're in and remember who you belong to.

_____

_____

_____

_____

_____

_____

_____

_____

_____

_____

_____

_____

OLLIEISM #4

Sometimes we're our own limitations so be mindful of the choices you make. It could be the difference between a lifetime of teachable but happy moments or a lifetime of blaming others.

✦ OLLIEISM #5 ✦

Self-inflicted wounds often result from unresolved life issues. To heal, it is essential to practice daily affirmations that cultivate self-love and self-acceptance, which are crucial for effective self-care.

⎯⎯⎯⎯⎯⎯•⎯⎯⎯⎯⎯⎯•⋗✦⋖•⎯⎯⎯⎯⎯⎯•

_____

_____

_____

_____

_____

_____

_____

_____

_____

_____

_____

_____

_____

✦ OLLIEISM #6 ✦

Don't overvalue material possessions because those things depreciate with time.

———•———•··●━➤❋◄━●··•———•———

_____

_____

_____

_____

_____

_____

_____

_____

_____

_____

_____

_____

_____

_____

_____

_____

✦ OLLIEISM #7 ✦

Don't permit those who are mentally shackled to negativity to be the rationale for your self-imposed imprisonment.

———•———••●⟩⟨⟩⟨●••———•———

_____

_____

_____

_____

_____

_____

_____

_____

_____

_____

_____

_____

_____

✦ OLLIEISM #8 ✦

Only God can make your house a home. When you make that purchase, join hands with your family and pray over your place of rest.

_____

_____

_____

_____

_____

_____

_____

_____

_____

_____

_____

_____

OLLIEISM #9

As humans, we tend to dedicate ourselves to our careers, driven by the need for financial security. Yet, it is imperative to recognize and value the individual who plays a pivotal role in our success. Our Lord and Savior!

✦ OLLIEISM #10 ✦

True love doesn't come with a price tag. Reflect on that.

_____

_____

_____

_____

_____

_____

_____

_____

_____

_____

_____

_____

_____

_____

_____

_____

_____

_____

✦ OLLIEISM #11 ✦

We are all seeds of the divine, planted in the earthly
garden of the most high. Each of us is nurtured by
his radiant sunlight and life-giving rain, allowing us
to flourish. Even amidst the most turbulent storms,
he doesn't uproot us; instead, God strengthens our
roots and deepens our resilience. Grow through
what you go through.

——————————•≫≪•——————————

_____

_____

_____

_____

_____

_____

_____

_____

_____

_____

✦ OLLIEISM # 12 ✦

Cultivating positive influences in the lives of others requires ongoing support. Therefore, strive to be a source of illumination during challenging times, utilizing adversity as a catalyst for growth

---

_____

_____

_____

_____

_____

_____

_____

_____

_____

_____

_____

_____

OLLIEISM #13

God designed your life with trials and tribulations on purpose so that you can appreciate the blessings you are receiving

---

✦ OLLIEISM #14 ✦

When you attain your peace, you will also attain purpose.

_____

_____

_____

_____

_____

_____

_____

_____

_____

_____

_____

_____

✦ OLLIEISM #15 ✦

Start each day with the intention of making a positive impact on someone's life and watch your blessings unfold.

———•———————••●➤⋇⋸●••———————•———

_____

_____

_____

_____

_____

_____

_____

_____

_____

_____

_____

_____

✦ OLLIEISM #16 ✦

New Season, new aspirations, new normal endeavor to be a blessing to as many people as you possibly can.

———— ••●➤✦◄●•• ————

_____

_____

_____

_____

_____

_____

_____

_____

_____

_____

_____

_____

_____

✦ OLLIEISM #17 ✦

Recognize the significance of small acts from loved ones, as these foster memories that will stand the test of time.

———————•••●➤》《◀●••——————

_____

_____

_____

_____

_____

_____

_____

_____

_____

_____

_____

_____

_____

✦ OLLIEISM # 18 ✦

Since love is not accompanied by receipts, it is not a commodity to be bought. Rather, it is a precious gift that affords countless opportunities for self-improvement. Thus, treasure those God brings into your life.

———————————————

_____

_____

_____

_____

_____

_____

_____

_____

_____

_____

_____

_____

✦ OLLIEISM #19 ✦

Genuine trust between the bottom and point
positions is essential for the triangle offense to be
effective. So, make God your focus and witness
blessings showering down like an April day.

———————————————————

_____

_____

_____

_____

_____

_____

_____

_____

_____

_____

_____

_____

_____

✦ OLLIEISM #20 ✦

Men, we are similar to cars, able to take women to their desired destinations. Nevertheless, we have to acknowledge that women are the keys, and we are unable to commence without them. Therefore, we must respect the strength of our queens for giving us drive.

✦ OLLIEISM #21 ✦

Be the best version of yourself every day.

✦ OLLIEISM #22 ✦

Social media can bring out the worst in people in their real lives. Therefore, it is essential not to get caught up in the distorted reality presented by individuals who post about a fake life.

———————•◦●➤✳︎❮●◦•———————

_____

_____

_____

_____

_____

_____

_____

_____

_____

_____

_____

_____

_____

OLLIEIS #23

Concentrate on attaining small daily successes during your healing process. Avoid placing excessive demands on yourself, which could lead to additional, unnecessary damage.

\
\
\
\
\
\
\
\
\
\
\
\
\
\
\

✦ OLLIEISM #24 ✦

The hardships you face in life are merely preparations for the blessings God has destined for you throughout your life's journey.

————•———•◦——◉⟩⟨◉——•◦———•————

_____

_____

_____

_____

_____

_____

_____

_____

_____

_____

_____

_____

_____

✦ OLLIEISM #25 ✦

As a youth, playing red light, green light was a fun experience. We didn't know that the principles of that game would be the ones we follow as adults. Sometimes your body is constantly on the go, and we ignore the signs to slow down or even stop. Allow yourself time for some much-needed rest to rejuvenate your body. Red light!

_____

_____

_____

_____

_____

_____

_____

_____

_____

_____

_____

✦ OLLIEISM #26 ✦

A woman should dress in accordance with how she wants to be addressed, and not undressed.

_____

_____
_____
_____
_____
_____
_____
_____
_____
_____
_____
_____
_____
_____

✦ OLLIEISM #27 ✦

MEN MATURITY IS MANDATORY! As the foundation, we must demonstrate to our community that we are solid.

_____

_____

_____

_____

_____

_____

_____

_____

_____

_____

_____

_____

_____

_____

✦ OLLIEISM #28 ✦

Stop disregarding God's notifications.

_____

✦ OLLIEISM #29 ✦

Raising the bar necessitates raising a moderate amount of hell.

———————·•●→⚹←●•·———————

_____

_____

_____

_____

_____

_____

_____

_____

_____

_____

_____

_____

_____

_____

_____

✦ OLLIEISM #30 ✦

If art mirrors life, what are you bringing to the
canvas? How does your work resonate with others?
Your unique artistic voice can inspire meaningful
change in both yourself and those around you.

✦ OLLIEISM #31 ✦

Once you have unlocked the hidden potential that has been dormant throughout your life, the standard by which you conduct yourself and influence those around you undergoes a profound transformation. Tapping into the purpose and design that God has intended for you revolutionizes your existence.

———————————————————

_____

_____

_____

_____

_____

_____

_____

_____

_____

_____

✦ OLLIEISM #32 ✦

Despite uncertain circumstances, God remains
a constant source of comfort, and His grace and
mercy are sufficient to see us through all situations.

_____

_____

_____

_____

_____

_____

_____

_____

_____

_____

_____

_____

_____

_____

✦ OLLIEISM #33 ✦

Be a guiding light for those who live in darkness. Be a mirror for those who need to recognize their own greatness.

———————————•••●⟩⦀⟨●•••———————————

_____

_____

_____

_____

_____

_____

_____

_____

_____

_____

_____

_____

_____

✦ OLLIEISM #34 ✦

Accountability is essential in a successful relationship, allowing for the respectful expression of concerns and emotions.

---

www.ingramcontent.com/pod-product-compliance
Lightning Source LLC
Chambersburg PA
CBHW050903120626
46554CB00003B/979